重要表現を身につけて失礼のない英語を身につけましょう

　本書は、*Useful English for Communication*（David E. ）
ロングセラー英語教材を改訂したものです。ロングセラーの
ながるという声を戴いた、シンプルながらもよく練られた構成と、

によく使われる失礼のない表現の的確さにあったと考えています。改訂に際しては、そうした特長はそのままに、登場人物の変更、ダイアログ内の話題のアップデート、練習問題の構成の一部変更をしました。

　日本の大学に通うリコとサクラが大学主催のアメリカでの語学研修に参加することになります。英語の習得のみならず異文化に触れて驚いたり疑問を感じたりするなど、等身大の大学生の目線に配慮したリアルな設定になっています。日本やアメリカの文化や社会、習慣にまつわる事情の違いに直面しながら、彼女たちがお互いに疑問に思うことを質問し合い、問題を提起する構成になっています。

　日本では毎日大学や学校で英語を日常的に使用しているケースはほぼ稀ですが、英語は日本から一歩外へ出れば、世界の共通語として使用されています。

　しかし、日本の大学の中でも、さまざまな国から留学しに来ている友人が周囲にたくさんいるでしょう。重要な文法や表現を確実に自分のものにして応用するすべを身につけ、英語でさまざまな国の人とやりとりをする中で、異文化を知り、より深く広い視野を身につけることは、これ以上ない生きる糧になります。

本書は 15 章構成で、
1 ダイアログ
2 ダイアログの一部の聞き取り
3 ダイアログで使用されている基本的かつ日常的表現法の確認
4 ダイアログで使用されている文法項目の復習と確認
5 ダイアログで使用された語・語句を使用しての基本的な英作文
6 ダイアログの内容を少し発展させた英作文（語句の整序問題になっているため、文構築の理解力が飛躍的に増大します）

という枠組みになっています。

Contents

1	Shall we go to America together to learn English?		譲歩の表現／受動態	03
2	I'm a little excited about the orientation!		相手をほめる表現／現在完了形（1）	07
3	Is it OK to use my smartphone to pay?		内容を確認する表現／助動詞	11
4	I'm planning to rent a suitcase from the rental shop.		推量する表現／関係代名詞	15
5	The captain of this plane is saying something!		不満を述べる表現／複文（1）	19
6	This form is an "Immigration form."		相手を誘う表現／複文（2）	23
7	How do you like the salad bars they have?		考えや希望を述べる表現／名詞節	27
8	How was your first class, Sakura?		受け答えの表現／to不定詞（1）	31
9	Mr. Carpenter said "grace" before eating.		聞き返しの表現／接続詞	35
10	English is a very important foreign language in Korea.		会話をつなぐ表現／現在分詞・動名詞	39
11	I had tacos for the first time in my life!		肯定・否定の表現／現在完了形（2）	43
12	It took me more than a week to prepare my presentation.		疑いを述べる表現／to不定詞（2）	47
13	They may sell these potatoes by the pound.		数量の表現／命令文	51
14	I've long wanted to visit Disneyland in America.		驚きの表現／再帰代名詞	55
15	I've made up my mind to study English harder.		意志や決心を述べる表現／代名詞	59

Shall we go to America together to learn English?

この章で学ぶこと　　譲歩の表現
受動態

Three weeks'
English study and
homestay in
America

次の会話を聴きましょう。　　　　🔊 **Audio 02**

Riko: Sakura, did you notice the colorful posters on the school bulletin board?

Sakura: No, I didn't. What are they about?

Riko: They are about "Three weeks' English study and homestay in America" during the summer vacation. This study is organized by our university.

Sakura: Then, our university is responsible for the program, isn't it?

Riko: Yes, it is. Also, we can get two credits for English Communication II. I'm thinking of joining this program this summer. Shall we go to America together to learn English and experience the American way of life?

Sakura: I'd like to go with you, but I don't like English. I'm interested in American culture, though. Let me think about it for a few days.

📋 Notes ▶ **bulletin board**：掲示板　▶ **~ be organized** ：〜が企画される
▶ **be responsible for ~**：〜に責任がある　▶ **credit**：単位

A Pick Up the Words

ダイアログを見ずに次の空欄を埋めなさい。 Audio 03

1. Our _____ is responsible for the program, _____ it?

2. We can _____ two credits _____ English Communication II.

3. I'm thinking of _____ this program this _____.

4. I don't like _____. I'm interested in American _____, though.

5. _____ me think about it for a _____ days.

B Useful Expressions

譲歩の表現を学びましょう。ペアになって発音してみましょう。 Audio 04

1. **A:** Shall we go shopping this afternoon?
   今日の午後ショッピングに行かない？

   B: I'd like to, but I'll be busy with work.
   行きたいけど、仕事が忙しいんだ。

2. **A:** How about having a party tomorrow evening?
   明日の夕方パーティを開くのはどう？

   B: That's a good idea. I have a meeting in the evening, though.
   いいアイデアね。夜は会議が入っているんだけどね。

3. **A:** What do you say we go for a walk in the morning?
   午前中に散歩に出かけるのはどう？

   B: OK, but I won't be ready until 11 o'clock.
   オッケー、でも 11 時までは無理だよ。

Check Grammar 受動態の復習

日本語を参考にして、空欄に適語を入れなさい。

1. あなたはあの映画に興味がありますか？

Are you _____ _____ that movie?

2. これらのポスターは、ある有名な芸術家によって描かれた。

These posters _____ drawn _____ a famous artist.

3. 英語は世界中で話されていますか？

_____ English _____ all over the world?

4. この古い手紙は私の祖父によって書かれた。

This old letter _____ written _____ my grandfather.

5. 私は彼の大成功に非常に驚いている。

I'm quite _____ _____ his big success.

D **Basic Composition**

日本語を英語にしましょう。音声を聴いて正解を確認しましょう。 🔊 **Audio 05**

1. 私たちのクラブは5人の学生によって結成された。

Our club _____ _____ _____ five students.

2. その会社は乗客の安全に責任がある。

The company _____ _____ _____ the safety
of the passengers.

3. 来月、北海道に引越しをしようと考えている。

I'm _____ _____ _____ _____ Hokkaido
next month.

4. 私はあの映画をあなたと一緒に見たい。

I _____ _____ _____ _____ that movie with
you.

5. 昨日外出しました。熱があったんですが。

I went out yesterday. I _____ _____ _____, though.

E Composition

次の①〜⑤の語・語句を並べかえて、日本語の意味に合うような英文を作りなさい。

1. 若い時に外国に行けば、あなたは視野を広げることができるかもしれない。

① be able to   ② if you go abroad   ③ your horizons
④ when you are young   ⑤ broaden

You may _____ .

2. 海外で英語を学ぶことは流行しているが、海外で勉強しようと思う最初の頃の決意を決して忘れてはいけない。

① but never forget   ② to study English abroad,
③ of studying abroad   ④ your initial determination   ⑤ fashionable

It is _____ .

3. 外国に行く時は、行く場所の治安について考えなければいけない。

① you have to think   ② of the place   ③ go to a foreign country,
④ you are going to visit   ⑤ about the security

When you _____ .

4. 旅費に関しては、多くの大学生はアルバイトをしながらお金をためようとする。

① many university students   ② working part-time
③ to save money,   ④ try   ⑤ travel expenses,

As for _____ .

5. 外国への旅では、あらゆることに積極的な態度をとり好奇心を持つことが重要である。

① to have a positive attitude   ② to a foreign country,
③ about everything   ④ it is important   ⑤ and curiosity

On a trip _____ .

I'm a little excited about the orientation!

 この章で学ぶこと 相手をほめる表現
現在完了形（1）

次の会話を聴きましょう。　　　　　　　　　　　　　　🎙 **Audio 06**

Riko: I'm happy we can go to America together this summer. Sakura, how are you going to get your traveling expenses ready?

Sakura: That's still a big problem. My father agreed to lend me the expenses, but I have to return them in two years. How about you?

Riko: Well, I have been working as a part-timer more than half a year, and I've already saved enough money for the language program.

Sakura: Riko, you are smart. By the way, we are supposed to attend three orientation sessions about the trip starting from tomorrow.

Riko: That's right. I'm a little excited about the orientation. Do you have a passport, Sakura?

Sakura: Passport? No. This is my first time to go abroad. How do I get one?

 ▶ **travel(ing) expense**：旅費　▶ **lend ~**：〜を貸す　▶ **smart**：賢い
▶ **be supposed to ~**：〜することになっている　▶ **session**：集まり

7

A Pick Up the Words

ダイアログを見ずに次の空欄を埋めなさい。 Audio 07

1. I'm _____ we can go to America _____ this summer.

2. How are you going to _____ your traveling expenses _____?

3. I have _____ working as a part-timer _____ than half a year.

4. I've already _____ enough money for the language _____.

5. We are supposed to _____ three orientation sessions about the _____.

B Useful Expressions

相手をほめる表現を学びましょう。ペアになって発音してみましょう。 Audio 08

1. **A:** Did you really solve this problem? You must be smart.
   この問題を本当に解いたの？　あなたは賢いに違いない。

   B: No, the computer solved it.
   いや、コンピュータが解いたんだよ。

2. **A:** The beef in this *sukiyaki* is awfully good.
   このすき焼きの牛肉はとてもおいしい。

   B: Thank you. You're a gourmet.
   ありがとう。あなたはグルメだね。

3. **A:** Good looking tie!
   かっこいいネクタイだね！

   B: Thank you. Do you like it?
   ありがとう。気に入った？

Check Grammar 現在完了形（1）の復習

日本語を参考にして、空欄に適語を入れなさい。

1. 私はすでにこの物語を読んだ。

I have ＿＿＿＿＿＿＿ ＿＿＿＿＿＿＿ this story.

2. あなたは富士山に登ったことがありますか？

Have you ＿＿＿＿＿＿＿ ＿＿＿＿＿＿＿ Mt. Fuji?

3. 私はまだ宿題を終えていない。

I ＿＿＿＿＿＿＿ finished my homework ＿＿＿＿＿＿＿.

4. 彼は今朝からずっと病気で寝ている。

He has ＿＿＿＿＿＿＿ sick in bed ＿＿＿＿＿＿＿ this morning.

5. 私の弟は 3 時間、YouTube をずっと見ている。

My brother has been ＿＿＿＿＿＿＿ YouTube ＿＿＿＿＿＿＿ three hours.

D **Basic Composition**

日本語を英語にしましょう。音声を聴いて正解を確認しましょう。 🔊 **Audio 09**

1. 私どものお客様のために 1 部屋準備しなければなりません。

I ＿＿＿＿＿＿＿ ＿＿＿＿＿＿＿ ＿＿＿＿＿＿＿ a room ＿＿＿＿＿＿＿ for our guest.

2. 彼は東京に 1 か月以上滞在した。

He ＿＿＿＿＿＿＿ ＿＿＿＿＿＿＿ Tokyo for ＿＿＿＿＿＿＿ ＿＿＿＿＿＿＿ a month.

3. まさかの時に備えてお金を貯めよう。

Let's save money ＿＿＿＿＿＿＿ ＿＿＿＿＿＿＿ ＿＿＿＿＿＿＿ ＿＿＿＿＿＿＿.

4. 彼女は今日の夕方 5 時に着くことになっていた。

She ＿＿＿＿＿＿＿ ＿＿＿＿＿＿＿ ＿＿＿＿＿＿＿ arrive at five this evening.

5. あなたのお父さんにそれをどのように説明するつもりですか？

How are you going to _____ _____ _____
your father?

E Composition

次の①～⑤の語・語句を並べかえて、日本語の意味に合うような英文を作りなさい。

1. アルバイトの目的は、お金を稼ぐことだけでなく、色々な人に出会う機会を持つことでもある。

① is ② but also to have opportunities ③ to meet various people
④ not only to earn money ⑤ of working part-time

The purpose _____.

2. 親が子供を、生涯において自立心を持つようにしつけることは簡単ではない。

① for parents ② not easy ③ to train their children
④ in their lives ⑤ to have independence

It is _____.

3. 海外での語学研修に関し、大学はオリエンテーションに高い価値を置いている。

① on the orientation ② usually put ③ a high value
④ universities ⑤ study-abroad programs,

In language _____.

4. 外国へ行く時は絶対パスポートが要る。それは大切な身分証明書である。

① an important ID card ② you need a passport ③ by all means
④ go to a foreign country,

When you _____. It is _____.

5. ビザは、あなたが訪れようとしている国にあなたが入国することを認める公的なスタンプである。

① is an official stamp ② to visit ③ you are going ④ to allow you
⑤ to enter the country

A visa _____.

Is it OK to use my smartphone to pay?

この章で学ぶこと ● 内容を確認する表現
助動詞

次の会話を聴きましょう。　　　　　　　　　　　　　🔊 **Audio 10**

Sakura: Riko, I have a question about money. Mr. Kimura said at the orientation yesterday that we had better use a credit card while we are abroad. But what about using our smartphones to pay?

Riko: I don't know about that. I guess we all have a smartphone, but I wonder if we can use it to pay everywhere.

Sakura: I read that 80% of shoppers use mobile phones in a physical store so I suppose that it is popular in some places.

Riko: Is that so? I didn't know that!

Sakura: Have you ever paid for things with your smartphone when you go shopping?

Riko: Oh no not me. To tell you the truth I don't even know how to do it. I've seen people do it in convenience stores though.

Sakura: Well, I'm interested to know. Let's go to Mr. Kimura and ask him about it.

 Notes　　▶ **shopper**：買い物客　　▶ **physical store**：実店舗、リアル店舗

A Pick Up the Words

ダイアログを見ずに次の空欄を埋めなさい。 🔊 **Audio 11**

1. We had _____ use a credit card _____ we are abroad.

2. What _____ _____ our smartphones to pay?

3. I _____ _____ we can use it to pay everywhere.

4. _____ _____ that it is popular in some places.

5. _____ you _____ paid for things with your smartphone?

B Useful Expressions

内容を確認する表現を学びましょう。ペアになって発音してみましょう。 🔊 **Audio 12**

1. **A:** We'll have no English class tomorrow.
   明日は英語の授業はないよ。

   B: Are you sure?
   本当に？

2. **A:** This ring is made of gold.
   この指輪は金で出来ているんだ。

   B: Is that so? I didn't know that.
   そうなの？　それは知らなかった。

3. **A:** You should go to his office and apologize.
   彼のオフィスに行って謝罪すべきです。

   B: Do you really think so?
   本当にそう思いますか？

Check Grammar 助動詞の復習

日本語を参考にして、空欄に適語を入れなさい。

1. 私は来年、妻とタイを訪れたい。

I'd _____ to visit Thailand with my _____ next year.

2. この部屋では靴を脱がねばなりません。

You _____ to take off your _____ in this room.

3. 彼は夕方私に電話をすると言った。

He said he _____ call me _____ in the evening.

4. 遅くなってきた。もう出なければいけません。

It's late. We _____ better get _____ now.

5. 納豆が好きでなければ、食べる必要はありませんよ。

You don't _____ to eat *natto* if you don't _____ it.

D **Basic Composition**

日本語を英語にしましょう。音声を聴いて正解を確認しましょう。 🔊 **Audio 13**

1. 今週は新入生全員に対するオリエンテーション週間です。

This week is _____ _____ for all the new students.

2. 彼は 20 歳とは言っても、まだ子供のようです。

_____ _____ he is twenty, he is _____ _____ a child.

3. あなたは車の運転ができないのですか？ 私もできません。

You can't drive? I _____ _____, _____.

4. 彼の古い自転車は私の自転車と同じです。

His old bicycle is _____ _____ _____ _____.

5. 午前中の電車はいつもこんなに混んでいる。

There's _____ _____ _____ _____
on the train in the mornings.

E Composition

次の①〜⑤の語・語句を並べかえて、日本語の意味に合うような英文を作りなさい。

1. 海外に出かけるとき、お金を持って行く方法については 3 つの選択肢がある。現金、
スマートフォン、そしてクレジット・カードである。

① you have three choices　② go abroad,
③ about how to take money with you.　④ and credit cards
⑤ Cash, smartphones

When you _____ .

2. クレジット・カードはまた、身分証明書としても役に立つので、外国に出発する前に
手に入れておいたほうが良い。

① as an ID card,　② for a foreign country.　③ also serves
④ before you leave　⑤ you had better get one

Since a credit card _____ .

3. 窃盗は日本よりも外国のほうがもっと頻繁に起こると考えるのは、正しいかもしれない。

① more often　② that theft will occur　③ in foreign countries
④ to think　⑤ than in Japan

You may be right _____ .

4. もし小銭かスマートフォンを持っていないと、あなたはバスに乗ることができなかっ
たり、有料トイレに行くことができなかったり、ホテルのベル・ボーイにチップをあ
げることができないかもしれない。

① or give a tip to a bellboy　② go into a pay toilet
③ you may not be able to get on a bus,　④ a small amount of cash or a
smartphone,　⑤ have

If you don't _____ .

I'm planning to rent a suitcase from the rental shop.

この章で学ぶこと 推量する表現
関係代名詞

次の会話を聴きましょう。 　　　　　　　　　　　　　　　　　🔊 **Audio 14**

Sakura: What I'm worried about is the things I'll take to America with me. Have you got a suitcase yet?

Riko: No, I haven't. But I think we need a suitcase, because we'll be in America for more than three weeks.

Sakura: A good suitcase will be expensive, I suppose.

Riko: Of course. So I'm planning to rent one from the rental shop near my house. The rental cost is about 5,000 yen a month. In addition, the suitcase is nearly brand-new, you know.

Sakura: Oh, that's splendid. Why don't you take me to that shop, too?

Riko: OK. I'll ask my father to take us to the shop in his car.

📋 Notes　▶ **in addition**：さらに　▶ **nearly**：ほぼ　▶ **brand-new**：新品の
▶ **splendid**：素晴らしい

A Pick Up the Words

Audio 15

ダイアローグを見ずに次の空欄を埋めなさい。

1. What I'm _____ about is the things I'll _____ to America with me.

2. A good _____ will be expensive, I _____.

3. I'm _____ to rent one from the rental shop _____ my house.

4. Why _____ you take me to that shop, _____?

5. I'll _____ my father to take us to the shop in his _____.

B Useful Expressions

Audio 16

推量する表現を学びましょう。ペアになって発音してみましょう。

1. **A:** How much is a new suitcase?
   新品のスーツケースっていくら？

   B: I guess it's more than 30,000 yen.
   ３万円以上はすると思うよ。

2. **A:** Look at that cloud! It'll probably rain soon.
   あの雲を見て！　多分すぐに雨が降るよ。

   B: Yes. I'll take an umbrella with me.
   うん。傘を持っていく。

3. **A:** They will be here tomorrow, I suppose.
   明日彼らはここにいると思う。

   B: Oh, how do you know?
   へえ、どうして知ってるの？

Check Grammar 関係代名詞の復習

日本語を参考にして、空欄に適語を入れなさい。

1. これは昨日私が駅で買った雑誌です。

This is the _____ I _____ at the station yesterday.

2. あちらに見える男性は伊藤さんです。

The _____ you _____ over there is Mr. Ito.

3. 私がバッグに入れているものをあなたに見せましょう。

I'll _____ you _____ I have in my bag.

4. 私が今したいことはこのゲームをすることです。

_____ I would like to do now is to _____ this game.

5. ベンチに座っている女性を知っていますか？

Do you know the _____ _____ is sitting on the bench?

D **Basic Composition**

日本語を英語にしましょう。音声を聴いて正解を確認しましょう。　🔊 **Audio 17**

1. 私は病気の弟のことを本当に心配している。

I'm _____ _____ _____ my sick brother.

2. 彼は 30 歳以上だと思いますが。

_____ _____ he is _____ _____ thirty years old.

3. さらに、私は九州で車を借りようと思っています。

_____ _____, I'm _____ _____ _____ a car in Kyushu.

4. あなたの帽子は新品のように見えますね。どこで買ったのですか？

Your hat _____ _____. Where did you _____ _____?

5. 来月その動物園にあなたを連れて行きましょう。

I'll _____ _____ _____ _____ _____
next month.

▣ Composition

次の①～⑤の語・語句を並べかえて、日本語の意味に合うような英文を作りなさい。

1. 海外に行く時はできるだけ荷物の数を減らすようにしましょう。

① go abroad,　② of your belongings　③ try to reduce　④ the number
⑤ as much as possible

When you _____.

2. あなたが滞在している町の店で日用品を買うことは、外国での良い経験の１つである。

① where you are staying　② to buy daily commodities
③ in the stores of the town　④ in a foreign country
⑤ of the good experiences

It is one _____.

3. すぐに再びスーツケースを使用する計画がなければ、レンタルショップで借りるのが
良いかもしれない。

① at a rental shop　② have plans　③ it may be better
④ to use a suitcase again soon,　⑤ to rent one

If you don't _____.

4. 機内では、手荷物はあなたの前の席の下に入れるか、頭上の荷物入れに入れることに
なっている。

① or in the overhead compartment　② your bag
③ under the seat in front of you,　④ you are supposed　⑤ to put

On the plane _____.

5. 荷物の重量制限があるので、空港で預けるスーツケースに注意してください。

① because　② at the airport,　③ about the suitcase
④ they have the luggage weight limit　⑤ you check

Please be careful _____.

5

The captain of this plane is saying something!

この章で学ぶこと 不満を述べる表現
複文 (1)

Good morning...

次の会話を聴きましょう。 📶 **Audio 18**

Riko: Finally we are on the plane. This is my first experience to be on a plane. I'm really excited.

Sakura: Me, too. Oh, this seat is a little small for me. Once I'm seated, I can't move. And the seat belt pinches me. I'm afraid I won't be able to put up with conditions like this for nine hours.

Riko: Sakura, take it easy. So, we have to put our bags under the seat in front of us! I see.

Sakura: Listen, Riko. The captain of this plane is saying something. He said "Good morning" "Welcome" and something. I couldn't understand what he said in English.

Riko: Me, neither. I think Mr. Kimura should have shown us an example of the captain's announcements at the orientation. But don't worry. We can ask a flight attendant anytime.

Notes ▶ **once ~**：一度～すると ▶ **pinch ~**：～をはさんで締め付ける
▶ **put up with ~**：～に我慢する ▶ **condition**：状態
▶ **take it easy**：（命令文で）興奮しないで ▶ **should have shown ~**：～を見せるべきだった ▶ **flight attendant**：飛行機の客室乗務員

A Pick Up the Words

ダイアログを見ずに次の空欄を埋めなさい。

🔊 Audio 19

1. This is my ＿＿＿＿＿＿ experience to be on a ＿＿＿＿＿＿.

2. I'm ＿＿＿＿＿＿ I won't be able to put up with conditions ＿＿＿＿＿＿ this for nine hours.

3. We have to ＿＿＿＿＿＿ our bags under the ＿＿＿＿＿＿ in front of us!

4. The ＿＿＿＿＿＿ of this plane is saying ＿＿＿＿＿＿.

5. Mr. Kimura ＿＿＿＿＿＿ have shown us an ＿＿＿＿＿＿ of the captain's announcements.

B Useful Expressions

不満を述べる表現を学びましょう。ペアになって発音してみましょう。

🔊 Audio 20

1. **A:** Excuse me. We're making a line here.
   すみませんが、私たちはここで列に並んでいます。

   B: Oh, I'm sorry.
   ああ、ごめんなさい。

2. **A:** I'm afraid this steak is tough.
   このステーキは固いのですが。

   B: I apologize. I'll bring a new one soon.
   申し訳ございません。新しいものをお持ちいたします。

3. **A:** How can I get there in an hour?
   どうすれば一時間でそこに着けますか？

   B: Take it easy.
   落ち着いてください。

Check Grammar　複文(1)の復習

日本語を参考にして、空欄に適語を入れなさい。

1. 京都の多くのお寺を訪れることができて私は嬉しかった。

I _____ happy I could _____ many temples in Kyoto.

2. 今日は日曜日なので、町の図書館は閉館している。

_____ it is Sunday today, the city library _____ closed.

3. 私は 10 歳の時、ピアノを弾き始めた。

I _____ playing the piano _____ I was ten years old.

4. あの男性を一度知ったら、あなたは彼のことを好きになるでしょう。

_____ you know that man, you'll like _____.

5. 彼はコンピュータを使いこなせるとあなたは思いますか？

_____ you think he can _____ the computer well?

D **Basic Composition**

日本語を英語にしましょう。音声を聴いて正解を確認しましょう。　　🔊 **Audio 21**

1. これが外国人と話をする私の初めての経験です。

_____ _____ _____ _____ _____ to talk with a foreigner.

2. 飛行機が完全に止まるまで、座席に座っていてください。

Remain seated _____ _____ _____ _____ _____ a complete stop.

3. 私たちはこの悪天候に耐えなければいけない。

We have to _____ _____ _____ this bad weather.

4. 彼は私が日本語で書いたことを理解することができなかった。

He couldn't _____ _____ _____ _____ in Japanese.

5. そのプロジェクトについて、あなたは私たちに尋ねるべきでした。

You _____ _____ _____ _____ about the project.

E Composition

次の①～⑤の語・語句を並べかえて、日本語の意味に合うような英文を作りなさい。

1. 「シートベルト着用」のサインが消えるまで、シートベルトを常に着用していなければ
いけない。

① the "Fasten Seat Belt" sign　② fastened　③ keep your seat belt
④ until　⑤ is turned off

You must always _____ .

2. ほとんど自由に動けないので、座席では居心地よく感じないかもしれない。

① you can hardly move freely　② your seat　③ because
④ uncomfortable　⑤ you may feel

In _____ .

3. 機内では空気は非常に乾燥するので、ソフトドリンクをたくさん飲んだほうが良い。

① the air becomes so dry　② the plane　③ a lot of soft drinks
④ you had better drink　⑤ that

In _____ .

4. 機内のトイレは無駄なスペースがないように作られている。どのような物が入れられ
ているか見てみよう。

① Try to see　② are put in them　③ what kind of items
④ in the plane　⑤ are built very compact.

Lavatories _____ .

5. 食事の主料理、あるいはソフトドリンクの選択について聞かれた時、躊躇しないで自
分の返事をはっきりと言おう。

① are asked　② do not hesitate
③ about the choice of your dinner entrée　④ or soft drink,
⑤ to give your answer clearly

When you _____ .

6

This form is an "Immigration form."

この章で学ぶこと  相手を誘う表現
複文(2)

次の会話を聴きましょう。　　　　　　　　　　　　　　　🔊 **Audio 22**

Riko: Sakura, what is it that the flight attendant is giving to some of the passengers?

Sakura: I have no idea, but let's say "please" and get one for each of us. We'll see.

Riko: OK. No problem. Excuse me. Please give us two. Thank you.

Sakura: Oh, I understand. This form is an "Immigration form." Mr. Kimura told us about this at the orientation. He said this is a very important form when we enter the U.S.

Riko: I see. Then, let's fill in the form in clear block letters.

Sakura: At the Immigration Counter, all we have to do is show our passport and this form. Am I right? Riko, tell me why they use the word "immigration" though we are not going to emigrate?

Riko: Don't ask me such a difficult question!

 Notes　▶ **immigration form**：入国カード　▶ **fill in ~**：～を記入する
　　　　　▶ **block letter**：活字体、ブロック体
　　　　　▶ **Immigration Counter**：入国審査カウンター　▶ **emigrate**：～へ移住する

A Pick Up the Words

ダイアログを見ずに次の空欄を埋めなさい。　　　　　　　　　　　🔊 **Audio 23**

1. Let's _____ "please" and get one for _____ of us.

2. He said this is a very _____ form when _____ enter the U.S.

3. Let's _____ in the form in _____ block letters.

4. _____ we have to do is _____ our passport and this form.

5. Don't _____ me such a difficult _____!

B Useful Expressions

相手を誘う表現を学びましょう。ペアになって発音してみましょう。　🔊 **Audio 24**

1. **A:** School is over. Let's go home.
   学校が終わった。家に帰ろう。

   B: Yes, let's. I hope the bus isn't crowded.
   うん、帰ろう。バスが混んでないといいな。

2. **A:** Why don't you join us for lunch?
   私たちとランチを一緒にしない？

   B: Thank you. I'll be with you in a minute.
   ありがとう。すぐに行くね。

3. **A:** What do you think of going to Osaka next Saturday?
   来週の土曜日大阪に行くのはどう？

   B: I'm afraid I can't go.
   残念だけど行けない。

Check Grammar 複文(2)の復習

日本語を参考にして、空欄に適語を入れなさい。

1. 大学は勉強をする所であると、私たちの先生は言った。

Our teacher _____ university is a place to _____.

2. あなたがいつ日本に着くか教えてください。

Please _____ me when you will _____ in Japan.

3. あなたがしなければいけないことは、決心することです。

_____ you have to do is to _____ up your mind.

4. 彼は高かったが、輸入車を買った。

He _____ an imported car, though it _____ expensive.

5. 彼がどのようにスケートのやり方を学んだか、あなたは知っていますか？

Do you _____ how he _____ to skate?

D **Basic Composition**

日本語を英語にしましょう。音声を聴いて正解を確認しましょう。　　🔊 **Audio 25**

1. 私が先日あなたのお姉さんに会ったのは奈良でした。

_____ _____ _____ Nara that _____ _____ your sister the other day.

2. 彼が冗談を言っているのが、あなたはすぐにわかりますよ。

You'll _____ _____ _____ that he is _____.

3. 忘れずに申込書にブロック体で記入してください。

_____ _____ _____ _____ the application form in _____ letters.

4. あなたがしなければいけないことは、ベストを尽くして待つことです。

_____ _____ _____ _____ do is do your best and wait.

5. 彼は私たちの会社を辞めたと理解してよいのですね？

Am I _____ _____ _____ that he _____ our company?

E Composition

次の①～⑤の語・語句を並べかえて、日本語の意味に合うような英文を作りなさい。

1. たいてい、入国審査官は黙ってあなたのパスポートと入国カードを確認し、入国の目的は尋ねない。

① and immigration form silently,　② into the country

③ your passport　④ and does not ask your purpose of entry　⑤ checks

Usually the Immigration officer _____.

2. 入国審査官があなたにパスポートを返してくれる時、「ありがとう」と言うことを忘れないでおこう。

① the Immigration officer　② "Thank you"　③ don't forget to say

④ to you,　⑤ returns your passport

When _____.

3. ベルトコンベアに乗って回ってくる多くの荷物の中から、自分の荷物を見つけ出すことは簡単ではない。

① on the carousel　② from among a lot of luggage　③ not easy

④ to spot your own luggage　⑤ going round

It is _____.

4. 税関の後で、空港にある外貨両替所に行きアメリカのお金を少し手に入れた方が良い。

① to go to the "Foreign Money Exchange"　② of U.S. currency

③ and get a small amount　④ it is better　⑤ in the airport,

After the Customs, _____.

5. 街の銀行の為替レートは信頼がおける。したがって心配なく金を交換できる。

① so you can exchange　② in the city　③ your money without
worry　④ in the banks　⑤ is trustworthy,

The exchange rate _____.

7

How do you like the salad bars they have?

この章で学ぶこと 考えや希望を述べる表現
名詞節

次の会話を聴きましょう。　　　　　　　　　　　🔊 **Audio 26**

Sakura: I like our "Quad" in the dormitory.

Riko: Me, too. Four of us share one room, but of course there are four beds, four desks, a rest-room and a shower in the room.

Sakura: One bad point is that we don't have so much privacy. I think we have to put up with the situation.

Riko: Privacy aside, I think meals in the dormitory are just fantastic. Think about the quality and quantity of the meals they serve and the price they charge.

Sakura: I like their buffet style. You can eat as much as you like.

Riko: How do you like the salad bars they have? They have a variety of fresh vegetables.

📋 **Notes**　▶ **Quad**：「クオッド」4人1部屋の寮の宿泊形態　▶ **dormitory**：寮
　▶ **rest-room**：トイレ　▶ **~ aside**：〜は別にして　▶ **fantastic**：素晴らしい
　▶ **quality**：質　▶ **quantity**：量　▶ **charge ~**：〜を請求する
　▶ **buffet style**：バイキング形式、ビュッフェ式　▶ **a variety of ~**：色々な〜

A Pick Up the Words

ダイアログを見ずに次の空欄を埋めなさい。

Audio 27

1. One _____ point is that we don't _____ so much privacy.

2. I think we _____ to put up _____ the situation.

3. I think _____ in the dormitory are _____ fantastic.

4. Think _____ the quality and quantity of the meals they _____.

5. _____ do you like the salad _____ they have?

B Useful Expressions

考えや希望を述べる表現を学びましょう。ペアになって発音してみましょう。Audio 28

1. **A:** Why are you opening the window?
   なんで窓を開けてるの？

   B: I thought I heard something.
   なんか聞こえたかと思ったの。

2. **A:** I lost my front-door key in the department store.
   デパートで玄関の鍵を失くした。

   B: Let's hope someone will find it.
   誰かが見つけてくれることを願おう。

3. **A:** I'm afraid I made a mistake.
   ミスしたんじゃないかと心配なんだ。

   B: Never mind. I'm sure you will do better next time.
   気にしないで。次回はきっと成績良くなるよ。

Check Grammar 名詞節の復習

日本語を参考にして、空欄に適語を入れなさい。

1. 彼は誰も自分のことを信じてくれないと思った。

He _____ _____ would believe him.

2. 問題なのは、あなたがいつも夜更かしをすることだ。

The _____ is you always sit up _____ at night.

3. 実は、私は2つの大学を卒業した。

The _____ is that I graduated _____ two universities.

4. 問題は、私たちが現在お金が不足していることだ。

The _____ is that we are _____ of money at present.

5. 私たちが彼を助けようという思いが、彼に勇気を与える。

The thought _____ we will help him _____ him courage.

D **Basic Composition**

日本語を英語にしましょう。音声を聴いて正解を確認しましょう。 🔊 **Audio 29**

1. 1つの良い点は、私たちはいつでもスマートフォンを使用できることです。

_____ _____ _____ _____ _____ we can use the smartphone any time.

2. 私たちは小さな家に住んでいるので、あまりプライバシーがない。

_____ _____ _____ in a small house, we don't _____ _____ _____.

3. 冗談はさておき、彼はよくやったと私は思う。

Joking _____, I think _____ _____ _____ a _____ _____.

4. 3,000円を支払うと、好きなだけ食べて、飲むことができる。

If you pay 3,000 yen, you can eat and drink _____ _____ _____ _____ _____.

5. 彼らはそのサンドイッチに対して私たちに 700 円請求した。

_____ _____ _____ _____ _____ for the sandwiches.

E Composition

次の①〜⑤の語・語句を並べかえて、日本語の意味に合うような英文を作りなさい。

1. もしあなたが寮に滞在すれば、食事についての不満はほとんど出ないだろう。なぜならば好きなだけ食べることができるからである。

① any complaints about meals,　② you may hardly have
③ because　④ at the dormitory,　⑤ you can eat as much as you like

If you stay _____.

2. もし外国の学生と部屋を共用するならば、コミュニケーションのために英語を使用しなければならないかもしれない。

① you may have to use　② for communication　③ English
④ with a foreign student,　⑤ share a room

If you _____.

3. 寮はたいてい昼食を出さない。私たちは外食をしなければならないが、さまざまなレストランで色々な食べ物を食べることができる。

① doesn't serve lunch.　② We have to eat out,
③ at different restaurants　④ a variety of foods
⑤ but we can experience

Usually the dormitory _____.

4. 一般的に寮では、土曜日と日曜日にはブランチとディナーを出してくれる。

① and Sundays　② brunch and dinner　③ they serve
④ on Saturdays　⑤ at the dormitory,

In general, _____.

5. 寮では門限の規則がある。しかし大学生は大人として扱われるので、門限は厳しく適応されていない。

① so the curfew is not imposed strictly　② are treated as adults,
③ a curfew.　④ they have　⑤ University students, however,

At the dormitory, _____.

How was your first class, Sakura?

Unit **8**

この章で学ぶこと ➡ 受け答えの表現
to 不定詞 (1)

次の会話を聴きましょう。　　　　　　　　　　　　　🔊 **Audio 30**

Riko: So, according to the placement test we had yesterday, you and I were put in the different basic groups. How was your first class, Sakura?

Sakura: Well, our teacher, Mr. Smith, talked to us slowly about the life in this town.

Riko: Did you understand what he said?

Sakura: I doubt it. I've never heard English for such a long time. I feel so tired. I hope this 15-minute break will make me alive again. How was your class?

Riko: Our teacher, Mr. Robinson, taught us how to greet people in English. Sakura, do you happen to know the meaning of the phrase "on top of the world?"

Sakura: No. What does it mean? And when is it used?

 Notes　▶ **placement test**：クラス分けテスト
▶ **I doubt it.**（= **I don't think so.**）：そうは思わない　▶ **break**：休憩
▶ **greet ~**：〜に挨拶をする　▶ **Do you happen to know ~ ?**：ひょっとして
〜を知っていますか？　▶ **on top of the world**：有頂天で

A Pick Up the Words

ダイアログを見ずに次の空欄を埋めなさい。

Audio 31

1. You and I were _____ in the different _____ groups.

2. Mr. Smith _____ to us slowly about the _____ in this town.

3. I've never _____ English for such a _____ time.

4. I hope this 15-minute _____ will make me _____ again.

5. Mr. Robinson _____ us how to greet _____ in English.

B Useful Expressions

受け答えの表現を学びましょう。ペアになって発音してみましょう。

Audio 32

1. **A:** I left my heart in San Francisco.
   私はサンフランシスコが懐かしい。

   B: You don't say!
   言わないで！

2. **A:** You said that we had to return to the dormitory at 5 pm!
   あなたは午後 5 時に寮に戻らないといけないって言ってたよね！

   B: I was just pulling your leg!
   あなたをからかっただけだよ！

3. **A:** We found he was telling a lie at that time.
   私たちは彼がその時嘘をついているとわかったよ。

   B: Is that so?
   そうなの？

Check Grammar to不定詞（1）の復習

日本語を参考にして、空欄に適語を入れなさい。

1. 朝早く起きることは私の習慣です。

_____ is my custom to get up _____ in the morning.

2. 彼は新しい機械の使い方を私たちに見せてくれた。

He _____ us how to _____ the new machine.

3. 私は iPad を持ってくるのを忘れました。

I forgot _____ bring my iPad _____ me.

4. 彼の楽しみは川に魚釣りに行くことです。

His pleasure is to _____ fishing in the _____.

5. 私は教室のどこに座るべきかわからなかった。

I didn't _____ where _____ sit in the classroom.

D **Basic Composition**

日本語を英語にしましょう。音声を聴いて正解を確認しましょう。　🔊 **Audio 33**

1. 今日の新聞によれば、5 人がその火事で亡くなった。

_____ _____ today's paper, five people died _____

_____ _____.

2. 今から 10 分間の休憩をとりましょう。

_____ _____ _____ _____ _____ from now.

3. 私がずっと収集しているものをあなたに見せましょう。

I'll show you _____ _____ _____ _____ _____.

4. 私は病院で偶然おばに会った。

_____ _____ _____ _____ my aunt in the hospital.

5. 私はその試験に合格したとき、有頂天になったように感じた。

When I passed the exam, I felt _____ _____ _____

_____ _____.

E Composition

次の①〜⑤の語・語句を並べかえて、日本語の意味に合うような英文を作りなさい。

1. 語学学校の 2 つのタイプのうち 1 つは、大学のキャンパスにある語学センターである。もう 1 つは街にある別個の語学センターである。

① of language school　② on the university campus.
③ is the language center
④ is the independent language center in the city　⑤ The other

One of the two types _____.

2. 大学のキャンパスにある語学センターは、図書館や学生ホールを利用できる利点がある。

① gives you the advantage　② to the library　③ or student hall
④ of having access　⑤ on the university campus

The language center _____.

3. 大学の語学センターでは、1 学期はたいてい 9-12 週間である。そして 1 日に 3、4 時間の授業がある。

① usually lasts for 9-12 weeks.　② the university language center,
③ And you'll have　④ 3 or 4 classes a day　⑤ one term

At _____.

4. 大学の語学センターで 10 週間の授業を申し込めば、授業料、寮費や日常生活費に約 70 万円が必要である。

① at the university language center,　② for the tuition, dormitory fee
③ you will need about 700,000 yen　④ and daily expenses
⑤ for a 10-week program

If you apply _____.

5. 一生懸命に英語を学ばなければ、どれほど多くお金を使っても、英語を習得することはできないだろう。

① you spend　② you won't be able to learn it
③ study English very hard,　④ how much money　⑤ no matter

If you don't _____.

Mr. Carpenter said "grace" before eating.

この章で学ぶこと 聞き返しの表現
接続詞

次の会話を聴きましょう。　　　　　　　　　　　　　　　🔊 Audio 34

Riko: Hi, Sakura! How was your homestay experience yesterday?

Sakura: Exciting! My host family were so casual. They treated me as if I were one of their family members.

Riko: How many members were there in your family?

Sakura: Just two. Mrs. Simpson and her daughter who is a junior high school student. Mrs. Simpson took us to a pizza shop for dinner. How was your experience?

Riko: There were three people. Mr. and Mrs. Carpenter and their son. He is ten years old. We had steak for dinner, but I was very surprised because Mr. Carpenter said "grace" before eating. Mrs. Carpenter and their son were praying silently.

Sakura: What did you say? "Grace?"

Riko: Yes, a prayer to thank God. I felt I was put in a completely different world.

📋 Notes　　▶ **grace**：（食前の）感謝の祈り　▶ **pray**：祈る　▶ **silently**：黙って
▶ **prayer**：祈り　▶ **completely**：完全に

A   Pick Up the Words

ダイアログを見ずに次の空欄を埋めなさい。　　　　　　　　　　🔊 Audio 35

1. How _____ your homestay _____ yesterday?

2. They treated me as _____ I were one of their _____ members.

3. Mrs. Simpson _____ us to a pizza shop for _____.

4. I was very _____ because Mr. Carpenter said "grace" before _____.

5. I _____ I was put in a completely different _____.

B   Useful Expressions

聞き返しの表現を学びましょう。ペアになって発音してみましょう。　　🔊 Audio 36

1. **A:** I beg your pardon?
    もう一度おっしゃってください。

   B: OK. Let me speak a little more slowly.
    わかりました。もう少しゆっくり話させてください。

2. **A:** Will you please say it again?
    もう一度言ってくれますか？

   B: Sure.
    わかりました。

3. **A:** I couldn't catch your name. Repeat it, please.
    お名前が聞き取れませんでした。もう一度言ってください。

   B: Carolyn Stokes.
    キャロリン・ストークスです。

Check Grammar 接続詞の復習

日本語を参考にして、空欄に適語を入れなさい。

1　春が来たが、まだ寒い。

Spring _____ come, _____ it is still cold.

2. 忙しかったので、残念ながらその本を読めませんでした。

I'm sorry I _____ read the book _____ I was busy.

3. 私たちは食べる前に手を洗う。

We _____ our hands _____ we eat.

4. あなたはジムに歩いて行くのですか、それとも自転車で行くのですか？

Are you _____ to the gym on foot _____ by bicycle?

5. あなたが出かけている間に誰かから着信がありましたよ。

Somebody _____ you up _____ you were out.

D **Basic Composition**

日本語を英語にしましょう。音声を聴いて正解を確認しましょう。　🔊 **Audio 37**

1. 中学校での教育実習はどうでしたか？

_____ _____ _____ teaching experience at junior high school?

2. 彼は私たちについてまるで何でも知っていたかのように話をする。

He talks _____ _____ _____ _____ _____ about us.

3. 私はあなたを明日、世界的に有名な水族館に連れて行きます。

_____ _____ _____ _____ the world-famous aquarium tomorrow.

4. 今日は夕食に本場のイタリアのスパゲティを食べますよ。

We'll _____ _____ Italian spaghetti _____ _____ today.

5. （食事の時に）トム、私たちのためにお祈りをしてくれますか？

Tom, will you _____ _____ _____ _____?

E Composition

次の①～⑤の語・語句を並べかえて、日本語の意味に合うような英文を作りなさい。

1. アメリカの家庭に滞在することは、アメリカの生活様式を学ぶ最善の方法の１つである。
① in an American home ② one of the best ways
③ about the American lifestyle ④ is ⑤ to learn
Staying _____.

2. 典型的なアメリカの家庭はない。なぜならばアメリカはさまざまな文化や習慣を持った移民で構成されているからである。
① America is made up of immigrants ② typical American home,
③ with different cultures ④ and customs ⑤ because
There is no _____.

3. ホームステイをしたら、滞在先の家庭の規則に従わなければいけない。
① follow ② of your family ③ the rules ④ you have to
⑤ with your host family,
When you stay _____.

4. ホームステイをしたら、あなたは自分でベッドを整え、部屋をきれいにすることを期待される。
① and clean ② you are expected ③ you homestay,
④ to make your own bed ⑤ your room yourself
When _____.

5. アメリカの家庭では、あなたを特別な客としてもてなさない。家族とコミュニケーションをとるためには、積極的な態度をとることを忘れないでおこう。
① to communicate with them ② treated
③ in your American family. ④ as a special guest
⑤ Don't forget to take a positive attitude
You will not be _____.

10 English is a very important foreign language in Korea.

この章で学ぶこと **会話をつなぐ表現**
現在分詞・動名詞

次の会話を聴きましょう。　　　　　　　　　　　　　🔊 **Audio 38**

Seo-yun: Welcome to my apartment! Come on in! These people are my Korean friends studying in this university. This is Kim Min-su, and that is Min In-ho.

Sakura: How do you do? My name is Yoshino Sakura. And this is my friend, Sawaki Riko. Nice to meet you.

Riko: I've never been to Korea, but my father has been to Pusan on business several times. He said many people in their 20's speak English.

Min-su: Oh, that's true. As you may know, English has become a very important foreign language in Korea. We study English very hard.

In-ho: You know, a lot of Koreans believe that speaking English will lead to success in life. Do lots of people speak English in Japan?

Sakura: I don't think so. We always speak Japanese.

📋 Notes　▶ **on business**：仕事で　▶ **20'**：20代　▶ **lead to ~**：〜に結びつく

39

A Pick Up the Words

ダイアローグを見ずに次の空欄を埋めなさい。 🔊 **Audio 39**

1. These people are my Korean _____ _____ in this university.

2. My father has _____ to Pusan on _____ several times.

3. He said many _____ in their 20's _____ English.

4. English has _____ a very important _____ language in Korea.

5. A lot of Koreans _____ that speaking English will lead to _____ in life.

B Useful Expressions

会話をつなぐ表現を学びましょう。ペアになって発音してみましょう。 🔊 **Audio 40**

1. **A:** You know, I sometimes feel I don't know him at all.
   あのね、私は時々彼のことがまったくわからないって感じるんだ。

   B: How come?
   どうして？

2. **A:** I'm already married, as you may know.
   ご存知かと思いますが、私は結婚しているんです。

   B: And I know you have two children.
   二人のお子さんもいらっしゃるでしょ。

3. **A:** By the way, you can stay for dinner, can't you?
   ところで、夕食の時間までゆっくりしていけるんでしょ？

   B: Thank you, but I have to go home by six o'clock.
   ありがとう。でも6時までに帰らなきゃ。

Check Grammar 現在分詞・動名詞の復習

日本語を参考にして、空欄に適語を入れなさい。

1. 庭で眠っている犬を見てごらん。

Look at the _____ _____ in the garden.

2. 私たちはたくさんの人が元気よく手を振っているのを見た。

We _____ many people waving their _____ cheerfully.

3. 百聞は一見にしかず、と言うのは本当です。

It is _____ that _____ is believing.

4. 私は午前中に公園を走るのが好きです。

I'm _____ of _____ in the park in the morning.

5. 私は銀行であの女性を見たのを覚えている。

I remember _____ that woman at the _____.

D **Basic Composition**

日本語を英語にしましょう。音声を聴いて正解を確認しましょう。 🔊 **Audio 41**

1. 門の所で座っている少年たちの写真を撮りなさい。

Take a photo of _____ _____ _____ _____ the gate.

2. あなたはこれまでに中国語か韓国語を勉強したことはありますか？

_____ _____ _____ _____ Chinese or Korean?

3. 昨年、私たちは仕事でヨーロッパに行った。

Last year _____ _____ to _____ _____ _____.

4. 70 代の人々はまだ元気いっぱいである。

_____ _____ _____ 70's are _____ full of vigor.

5. この大学を卒業することが出世につながるかもしれない。

_____ from this university _____ _____ _____ a career.

E Composition

次の①～⑤の語・語句を並べかえて、日本語の意味に合うような英文を作りなさい。

1. 語学センターには、たいてい色々な国出身の学生がいる。彼らと友達になるようにしよう。

① usually there are students   ② Try   ③ from various countries.
④ with some of them   ⑤ to become friends

In the language center, _____.

2. パーティに招待された時は、参加する前にどのようなパーティであるかを知ることが重要である。

① to know   ② before joining it   ③ what kind of party it is
④ it is important   ⑤ to a party,

When you are invited _____.

3. パーティでは、話しかけられるまで待っていてはいけない。積極的な態度で他の人に話しかけなければいけない。

① to others   ② until you are spoken to.   ③ with a positive attitude
④ don't wait   ⑤ You must try to speak

At the party, _____.

4. 世界の多くの国で、英語は科学技術、経済や教育の発展になくてはならない言語である。

① economy and education   ② in the world,
③ of science and technology,   ④ English is an indispensable language
⑤ for the development

In many countries _____.

5. 日本では日常のコミュニケーションに英語は要らないが、小学校に英語教育を導入することを主張する人もいる。

① on the introduction of teaching English
② for our daily communication,   ③ we don't need English
④ but some people insist   ⑤ at elementary school

In Japan, _____

11

I had tacos for the first time in my life!

この章で学ぶこと　肯定・否定の表現
現在完了形(2)

次の会話を聴きましょう。　　　　　　　　　🔊 **Audio 42**

Riko: Every day we've been looking for a restaurant in the Food Court to try different foods for lunch.

Sakura: Yes. So far we've visited Chinese, Italian, Korean, and Vietnamese restaurants.

Riko: What was the name of the food we had at the Mexican restaurant? Something like fried, thin crust filled with meat and beans.

Sakura: Oh, that's a taco. That was the first time I had tacos in my life. Did you like it?

Riko: Not as much as McDonald's hamburgers. By the way, what's your favorite American food?

Sakura: Hot dogs. Especially I like sausages. How about your favorite American food?

Riko: Ice cream. Ice cream here in America is just delicious.

 ▶ **food court**：「フード・コート」ショッピング・モールや空港で色々な飲食店が集まり、共通の客席を持っている広場　▶ **thin crust**：クリスピー・タイプの
▶ **filled with ~**：〜でいっぱいの　▶ **favorite**：好きな　▶ **especially**：特に

A Pick Up the Words

ダイアログを見ずに次の空欄を埋めなさい。　　　　　🔊 **Audio 43**

1. Every day _____ been _____ for a restaurant in the Food Court.

2. What was the _____ of the food we _____ at the Mexican restaurant?

3. That was the _____ time I had tacos in my _____.

4. By the _____, what's your _____ American food?

5. _____ cream here in America is just _____.

B Useful Expressions

肯定・否定の表現を学びましょう。ペアになって発音してみましょう。　　　🔊 **Audio 44**

1. **A:** Did you try roast beef in England?
   イギリスでローストビーフは食べた？

   B: Yes, of course. It was just wonderful.
   うん、もちろん。実においしかった。

2. **A:** How do you like coconut milk?
   ココナッツミルクは気に入った？

   B: Well, to tell the truth, I don't like it so much.
   いやあ、実は、あまり好きじゃないんだ。

3. **A:** I have never realized hot dogs are this tasty.
   ホットドッグがこんなにおいしいなんて思ってもいなかった。

   B: I'm glad you love them.
   気に入ってくれてよかった。

Check Grammar 現在完了形（2）の復習

日本語を参考にして、空欄に適語を入れなさい。

1. 私は 2 時間本を読んでいる。

I _____ been reading a book _____ two hours.

2. これまでのところ、このあたりの 2、3 の山に登った。

So far we have _____ a few mountains around _____.

3. 私は小さな子供の頃からスミスさんを知っている。

I have _____ Mr. Smith _____ I was a little child.

4. あなたは今までメキシカン・レストランに行ったことがありますか？

Have you _____ been _____ a Mexican restaurant?

5. 子供たちはもう学校に行きましたか？

Have the children _____ to school _____?

D **Basic Composition**

日本語を英語にしましょう。音声を聴いて正解を確認しましょう。　🔊 **Audio 45**

1. 私のコンタクトレンズを探すのを手伝ってくれませんか？

_____ _____ _____ _____ look for my contact lens?

2. 今のところ、私たちは彼から一銭も借りていません。

_____ _____ _____ _____ not borrowed any money from him.

3. その悲しいお話を聞いて、彼女の目は涙でいっぱいだった。

_____ _____ _____ _____ _____ tears to hear the sad story.

4. 彼らは 1 年前ほどにはテレビを見ない。

They don't watch TV _____ _____ _____ they did a year ago.

5. 気分転換にお茶を一杯いかがですか？

_____ _____ _____ _____ _____ _____ for a change?

E Composition

次の①～⑤の語・語句を並べかえて、日本語の意味に合うような英文を作りなさい。

1. アメリカでは、さまざまな文化的背景に満ちた色々な種類の食べ物がある。

① of foods　② you will find　③ with different cultural backgrounds
④ various kinds　⑤ which are filled

In the U.S. _____.

2. 食べ物を注文し、代金を支払い、自分でテーブルに持っていく店では、チップは不要だ。

① in a shop　② by yourself　③ and carry it to your table
④ pay for it　⑤ where you order your food,

Tips are not necessary _____.

3. レストランに入る時は、入り口で立ち止まり、同伴者の人数をウェイトスタッフに言わねばならない。

① you must make a stop　② at the entrance,　③ and tell the waitstaff
④ the number of your party　⑤ into a restaurant,

When you go _____.

4. 外国で日本人は米を食べると元気をすぐに取り戻す、というのは本当だと思いますか？

① Japanese people will soon recover　② their vigor　③ it true
④ when they eat rice in a foreign country　⑤ that

Do you think _____?

5. アメリカでポップコーンやフレンチフライを注文すると、お皿の上のその量に驚くかもしれない。

① you may be surprised　② in the U.S.,　③ at the quantity
④ popcorn or French fries　⑤ on your plate

When you order _____.

12

It took me more than a week to prepare my presentation.

この章で学ぶこと 疑いを述べる表現
to不定詞 (2)

次の会話を聴きましょう。　　　　　　　　　　　　🔊 **Audio 46**

Mr. Robinson: Thank you very much for your presentation, Riko. It was very interesting.

Riko: This was the first time for me to give a presentation with PowerPoint. It took me more than a week to prepare my presentation about my university life in Japan.

Mr. Robinson: You have done a good job, Riko. I have one question for you. Do the university students study hard?

Riko: Well, some students study hard, of course. But for many students, university life seems like paradise. Most of my friends come to university to make friends, exchange information and have fun.

Mr. Robinson: Oh. Then, what will happen to those students who study?

Riko: We have a graduate school on campus. This is the place for them to study.

Mr. Robinson: I can't believe it!

📋 **Notes** ▶ **give a presentation**：発表をする ▶ **do a good job**：うまくやる
▶ **paradise**：天国 ▶ **graduate school**：大学院

A Pick Up the Words

ダイアログを見ずに次の空欄を埋めなさい。 Audio 47

1. This was the first _____ for me to _____ a presentation.

2. It _____ me more than a week to _____ my presentation.

3. For many students, _____ life seems _____ paradise.

4. My friends come to university to _____ friends, exchange _____ and have fun.

5. What will _____ to those students _____ study?

B Useful Expressions

疑いを述べる表現を学びましょう。ペアになって発音してみましょう。 Audio 48

1. **A:** The police will arrest Bill for drunk driving.
   警察はビルを飲酒運転で逮捕するでしょう。

   B: That's very unlikely.
   それはまずあり得ないでしょう。

2. **A:** My husband broke his leg yesterday.
   昨日私の夫が脚の骨を折ったの。

   B: No kidding!
   本当に？

3. **A:** She won first prize in the speech contest.
   彼女はスピーチコンテストで優勝したんだ。

   B: I can't believe it.
   本当？

Check Grammar to不定詞（2）の復習

日本語を参考にして、空欄に適語を入れなさい。

1. 彼女はそんなことをする女性ではない。

She is not a ＿＿＿＿＿＿ ＿＿＿＿＿＿ do such a thing.

2. 私たちは外国人とコミュニケーションをとるために英語を勉強する。

We ＿＿＿＿＿＿ English to communicate ＿＿＿＿＿＿ foreigners.

3. 大阪には訪れるのに面白い場所がたくさんある。

Osaka ＿＿＿＿＿＿ a lot of interesting places to ＿＿＿＿＿＿.

4. 昼食をとるために、このレストランに寄りましょう。

Let's drop ＿＿＿＿＿＿ at this restaurant ＿＿＿＿＿＿ have lunch.

5. 1時間目の授業に遅れないよう急がなければいけない。

We must hurry ＿＿＿＿＿＿ to miss the first period ＿＿＿＿＿＿.

D **Basic Composition**

日本語を英語にしましょう。音声を聴いて正解を確認しましょう。　🔊 **Audio 49**

1. 誕生日の贈り物、どうもありがとうございました。

＿＿＿＿＿＿ ＿＿＿＿＿＿ ＿＿＿＿＿＿ ＿＿＿＿＿＿ ＿＿＿＿＿＿ your birthday present.

2. 英語で発表するのはこれが2回目でした。

This was ＿＿＿＿＿＿ ＿＿＿＿＿＿ ＿＿＿＿＿＿ that I ＿＿＿＿＿＿ ＿＿＿＿＿＿ ＿＿＿＿＿＿ in English.

3. ここから空港に行くのに約30分かかるでしょう。

＿＿＿＿＿＿ ＿＿＿＿＿＿ ＿＿＿＿＿＿ about 30 minutes to ＿＿＿＿＿＿ ＿＿＿＿＿＿ the airport from here.

4. その手紙はほとんどフランス語で書かれていた。

＿＿＿＿＿＿ ＿＿＿＿＿＿ ＿＿＿＿＿＿ ＿＿＿＿＿＿ were written in French.

5. やはり、その少年たちは良い生徒のようだ。

After all, those boys ＿＿＿＿＿＿ ＿＿＿＿＿＿ ＿＿＿＿＿＿ ＿＿＿＿＿＿.

E Composition

次の①〜⑤の語・語句を並べかえて、日本語の意味に合うような英文を作りなさい。

1. 日本の高等教育進学率は、2019 年には 54.7% であった。これは高等学校卒業生の 2 人に 1 人が大学生であることを意味する。

① was 54.7% in 2019　② This means
③ one out of every two high school graduates
④ is a university student　⑤ to higher education in Japan

The rate of going _____.

2. もし大学が高等学校の教科の復習に強く焦点を合わせるならば、学生は勉強における関心を次第になくすかもしれない。

① lose their interest　② students may gradually　③ on doing reviews
④ in studying　⑤ of high school subjects,

If universities strongly focus _____.

3. 大学生の最大の利点は、彼らには自己を発展させ、研究を深める自由な時間が多くあることである。

① they have a lot of free time　② and deepen their study
③ to develop their own self　④ for university students　⑤ is that

The greatest advantage _____.

4. 大学生の時、少なくとも次の 3 つの外国語——英語、中国語、韓国語——の 1 つを学ぶことは、あなたの将来に役立つかもしれない。

① for your future
② at least, one of the following three foreign languages
③ while you are a university student　④ —English, Chinese or
Korean—　⑤ to learn,

It may be useful _____.

5. 日本の大学は、まもなく 2 つのグループに分けられるだろう。1 つのグループは教育を重視し、もう 1 つは研究を重視するグループである。

① will focus on research　② will soon be divided　③ and the other
④ into two groups.　⑤ One group will emphasize education,

Universities in Japan _____.

They may sell these potatoes by the pound.

この章で学ぶこと  **数量の表現**
命令文

次の会話を聴きましょう。　　　　　　　　　　　　 🔊 **Audio 50**

Sakura: So, this is an American supermarket. What a huge parking lot! Let's go in.

Riko: Look at these fresh vegetables. Look at these big "Peamans!" I wonder how Americans eat them.

Sakura: Riko, look at the name tag. Their name isn't "peamans." It says "Green peppers."

Riko: I see. What does "lb" mean, by the way? Look, here, potatoes.

Sakura: I'm not sure, but I suppose they may sell these potatoes by the pound, not by the kilo.

Riko: A weight unit? What is a pound in kilos, then?

Sakura: Let me check my dictionary. Er... it says a pound is about 454 grams.

Riko: What a complicated weight unit!

 Notes ▶ **huge**：巨大な　▶ **lb** = libra = pound：重量ポンド　▶ **by the pound**：ポンド単位で　▶ **er**：えー、あのー　▶ **complicated**：複雑な、わかりにくい

A Pick Up the Words

ダイアログを見ずに次の空欄を埋めなさい。

Audio 51

1. I _____ how Americans eat _____.

2. _____ does "lb" mean, by the _____?

3. I suppose they may _____ these potatoes _____ the pound.

4. What is a pound in _____, _____?

5. _____ a complicated weight _____!

B Useful Expressions

数量の表現を学びましょう。ペアになって発音してみましょう。

Audio 52

1. **A:** How much sugar do you want?
   砂糖はどれくらい欲しい？

   B: I want two spoonfuls.
   スプーン 2 杯分。

2. **A:** How many pounds does your dog weigh?
   あなたの犬の体重は何ポンド？

   B: He usually weighs 66 pounds but he has gained 10 pounds recently.
   彼はたいてい体重は 66 ポンドだけど、最近 10 ポンド増えたんだ。

3. **A:** My son is three feet six inches. How tall is your son?
   僕の息子は 3 フィート 6 インチなんだ。君の息子の背は何センチ？

   B: He is about three feet tall.
   3 フィートくらいだよ。

Check Grammar 命令文の復習

日本語を参考にして、空欄に適語を入れなさい。

1. 出かける前に窓を閉めなさい。

_____ the window _____ you go out.

2. 教室では騒がしくしてはいけません。

_____ _____ noisy in the classroom.

3. 車のキーを持ってくるのを忘れないでください。

Don't _____ to _____ the car key with you.

4. あなたの新しい時計を私に見せてください。

_____ me have a look _____ your new watch.

5. 今起きなさい、そうすればバスに間に合いますよ。

_____ up now, _____ you'll be in time for the bus.

D **Basic Composition**

日本語を英語にしましょう。音声を聴いて正解を確認しましょう。　　🔊 **Audio 53**

1. なんて素敵なボートを持っているのでしょう！　うらやましいですね。

_____ _____ _____ _____ you have! I envy you.

2. 「vegan」という言葉の意味は何ですか？

_____ _____ the word "vegan" _____?

3. 私は時給でこの事務所に雇われている。

I'm _____ in this office _____ _____ _____.

4. 日本では肉はたいていグラム単位で売られている。

Meat is usually _____ _____ _____ _____ in Japan.

5. 彼女に電話をしても、彼女は今はあなたの電話に出ないかもしれない。

She _____ _____ answer your call now _____ _____ you call her.

E Composition

次の①～⑤の語・語句を並べかえて、日本語の意味に合うような英文を作りなさい。

1. この箱のアイスクリームは、ガロン単位で売られている。1/2 ガロンはミリリットルでどのくらいか教えてくれませんか？

 ① Can you tell us ② in mls? ③ "a half gallon" is ④ how much
 ⑤ is sold by the gallon.

This box of ice cream _____?

2. 外国の町のスーパーに立ち寄れば、その地域の生活様式の知識を得られるかもしれない。

 ① at a supermarket ② you may get an idea
 ③ in a city in a foreign country, ④ of that area ⑤ of the lifestyle

If you drop in _____.

3. アメリカでは、「並ぶ」ということは非常に重要な社会の規則である。人々は自分の順番が来るまで、長い間、辛抱強く待っている。

 ① for a long time ② until their turn comes around
 ③ making a line ④ People wait patiently
 ⑤ is a very important social rule.

In the U.S., _____.

4. アメリカのスーパーでは長さの異なる小さな人参が、同じお皿に盛られ、売られている。

 ① are often put together ② of different length
 ③ in the U.S. supermarket ④ on the same plate ⑤ to sell

Small carrots _____.

5. アメリカのスーパーは、たいてい街の郊外にあり、1日24時間営業している。

 ① 24 hours a day ② in the suburbs ③ and are open
 ④ are usually located ⑤ of the city,

Supermarkets in the U.S. _____.

14 I've long wanted to visit Disneyland in America.

この章で学ぶこと  驚きの表現
再帰代名詞

次の会話を聴きましょう。　　　　　　　　　　　　　　🔊 **Audio 54**

Sakura: Now, we are back at our hotel. What time is it? Wow, it's already 11:30. I'm very happy I could enjoy myself so much at Disneyland until late in the evening.

Riko: Me, too. I've long wanted to visit Disneyland in America. I'm glad I could come to America.

Sakura: Riko, did you notice that at Disneyland people of different ages were enjoying themselves together?

Riko: Yes. I had an impression that they seemed to be having fun, and relaxing at Disneyland.

Sakura: By the way, how did you like the Electrical Parade? I was completely taken into a fantasy and dream world.

Riko: And the Paradise of Dreams! Wasn't that fantastic? I'll never forget the memory of this wonderful evening.

 Notes　▶ **notice ~**：〜に気づく　▶ **impression**：印象

A Pick Up the Words

ダイアログを見ずに次の空欄を埋めなさい。 〰 **Audio 55**

1. I could _____ myself so much at Disneyland until _____ in the evening.

2. I've _____ _____ to visit Disneyland in America.

3. At Disneyland people of different _____ were enjoying themselves _____.

4. I was completely _____ into a fantasy and dream _____.

5. I'll _____ forget the _____ of this wonderful evening.

B Useful Expressions

驚きの表現を学びましょう。ペアになって発音してみましょう。 〰 **Audio 56**

1. **A:** I failed the driving test again.
   また運転免許試験に落ちたんだ。

   B: That's too bad. Try once again.
   それは残念だったね。また受けてみなよ。

2. **A:** I was elected chairman of the meeting.
   私はその会議の議長に選ばれたんです。

   B: How wonderful!
   すごい！

3. **A:** My goodness, you spent a lot of money in Tokyo.
   やれやれ、東京で大金を使ったわね。

   B: I'm sorry. I'll try to save money from today.
   ごめん。今日からお金を節約するよ。

C Check Grammar 再帰代名詞の復習

日本語を参考にして、空欄に適語を入れなさい。

1. 山田さんは「歴史はくり返す」と言った。

Mr. Yamada said, "_____ repeats _____."

2. 彼女はそんな誤りをおかしたので、恥ずかしいと思っていた。

As she _____ such a mistake, she was ashamed of

_____.

3. 彼は 1 人で大きな家に住んでいる。

He _____ in a big house by _____.

4. その外国人に私の英語は通じない。

I can't make _____ _____ to the foreigner in English.

5. 海外に行く時は、身体に気をつけてください。

Please take care of _____ when you go _____.

D Basic Composition

日本語を英語にしましょう。音声を聴いて正解を確認しましょう。　📶 **Audio 57**

1. あなたが無事に家に帰ってきて、私はうれしい。

_____ _____ _____ _____ _____ home
safe and sound.

2. 私は、こういうアルバムを長い間欲しいと思っていた。

_____ _____ _____ _____ have an album
_____ _____.

3. 私たちはここでは必要とされていない、という印象を私は持っている。

_____ _____ _____ _____ _____ we are
not wanted here.

4. 新しく来られた私たちの先生はいかがでしたか？

_____ _____ _____ _____ our new teacher?

5. 一瞬にして私たちはマジックの世界に連れて行かれた。

In an instant _____ _____ _____ _____ a
magic world.

E Composition

次の①〜⑤の語・語句を並べかえて、日本語の意味に合うような英文を作りなさい。

1. 語学センターで勉強している期間、気分転換で小旅行に行くことは価値のあることである。

① to go on a short trip　② at the language center

③ for a change of air　④ you are studying　⑤ while

It is worthwhile _____.

2. 語学センターでは土曜日と日曜日には授業がないので、これらの日を利用する計画を立てることは賢明なことである。

① it is wise　② to make the best of these days　③ to make plans

④ does not teach you　⑤ on Saturdays and Sundays,

Since the language center _____.

3. アメリカで車を借りる時には、日本で発行された運転免許証と国際運転免許証を見せなければいけない。

① your driver's license　② a car in the U.S.,

③ and your international driver's license　④ issued in Japan

⑤ you must show

When you rent _____.

4. レンタカーのスピードメーターはしばしばマイル表示になっている。60 マイル／時は約 96 キロ／時である。スピードの出しすぎに注意するようにしましょう。

① about driving too fast　② Try to be careful　③ often reads in miles.

④ is about 96km/h.　⑤ 60 miles/h

The speedometer in a rent-a-car _____.

5. レンタカーを返す時は、ガソリンを満タンにすることを忘れないように。

① to fill it up　② your rent-a-car,　③ do not forget　④ with gas

⑤ you return

When _____.

I've made up my mind to study English harder.

この章で学ぶこと  意志や決心を述べる表現
代名詞

次の会話を聴きましょう。　🔊 **Audio 58**

Mr. Kimura: Our three-week study tour has nearly come to an end. How have you found our study and new experiences in the U.S.? How about you, Sakura?

Sakura: For me, it was very exciting to do research on the comparison of American newspapers and Japanese newspapers. I've never done this before.

Mr. Kimura: And everybody had to make a presentation by PowerPoint. I couldn't believe it. Now everybody, do you think your English has improved?

Riko: I think my listening ability has improved a little. I'm getting used to American pronunciation. I've made up my mind to study English harder when I go back to Japan.

Mr. Kimura: Well, I'm glad to hear it, and don't forget what you have just said.

Riko: No, I won't. I'm really serious.

 Notes　▶ **nearly**：ほぼ　▶ **do research on ~**：～について研究する
▶ **comparison**：比較　▶ **~ improve**：～が上達する　▶ **get used to ~**：～
に慣れる　▶ **pronunciation**：発音　▶ **make up one's mind to ~**：～する
ことを決心する　▶ **serious**：本気で

59

A Pick Up the Words

ダイアログを見ずに次の空欄を埋めなさい。

Audio 59

1. Our three-week study _____ has nearly _____ to an end.

2. It was _____ to do research on the comparison of American newspapers and _____ newspapers.

3. Now _____, do you think your English has _____?

4. I've made up my _____ to study English _____.

5. _____ forget what you have just _____.

B Useful Expressions

意志や決心を述べる表現を学びましょう。ペアになって発音してみましょう。 Audio 60

1. **A:** I'm thinking of becoming an actor in the future.
   僕は将来俳優になろうと考えてるんだ。

   B: What kind of actor do you mean?
   どんな俳優を目指してるの？

2. **A:** We're planning to have a farewell party for you.
   あなたの送別会を開く予定でいます。

   B: Thank you. When will it be?
   ありがとうございます。いつになりますか？

3. **A:** I've made up my mind to go up to Tokyo by plane.
   飛行機で東京に行くことに決めたよ。

   B: But the Shinkansen is faster than a plane.
   でも新幹線のほうが飛行機より速いよ。

C Check Grammar 代名詞の復習

日本語を参考にして、空欄に適語を入れなさい。

1. この池で泳ぐのは危険だ。

_____ is dangerous to _____ in this pond.

2. 私たちが科学を勉強することが重要である。

It is _____ _____ we should study science.

3. 私を助けることをあなたの義務と感じないでください。

Please don't feel _____ your duty _____ help me.

4. 彼がそのような質問をしたのは当然だと私は思います。

I think _____ natural _____ he asked such a question.

5. 覆水盆に返らず（こぼれた牛乳を嘆いてもどうにもならない）。

_____ is no use crying _____ spilt milk.

D Basic Composition

日本語を英語にしましょう。音声を聴いて正解を確認しましょう。 🔊 **Audio 61**

1. もう少しで正午です。お昼にしましょう。

_____ _____ twelve o'clock. Let's _____ _____.

2. 私は卒業論文の研究をまだやっています。

I'm _____ _____ _____ for my graduation thesis.

3. あなたの九州旅行について発表してくれませんか？

Will you _____ _____ _____ _____ your trip to Kyushu?

4. 私たちはその新しい習慣にどんどん慣れてきている。

We're _____ _____ _____ the new custom.

5. やろうと決心したことを実行しましょう。

Let's carry out what we have _____ _____ _____ _____ to do.

E Composition

次の①〜⑤の語・語句を並べかえて、日本語の意味に合うような英文を作りなさい。

1. 3週間の語学研修では英語があまり上達しないが、この研修は英語を学ぶ重要性にきっと気づかせてくれる。

① make you notice　② does not improve　③ the importance of learning English　④ your English much,　⑤ but it will surely

Three weeks' language study _____.

2. 海外の語学研修の大きな利点の1つは、文化の相違を直接経験できることである。

① you can have　② of cultural differences　③ a direct experience
④ is that　⑤ of language study abroad

One of the great advantages _____.

3. もし英語を集中的に6-9か月間、強く決心し努力して学べば、間違いなく英語を上達させることができる。

① you can improve your English　② intensively for 6-9 months
③ and effort,　④ without fail　⑤ with your strong determination

If you learn English _____.

4. 英語を上達させるためには、英文法の知識と豊富な語彙が必要であることを忘れないことである。

① of English grammar　② in order to improve
③ that you need a knowledge　④ and rich vocabulary　⑤ your English

Don't forget _____.

5. 授業で学生の英語を上達させる1つの方法は、先生ができるだけ英語を話すようにすることである。

① as often as possible　② in class　③ is that　④ the students' English
⑤ the teacher should try to speak English

One way to improve _____.

English Expression Pre-Intermediate

コミュニケーションのための英語表現レッスン：自己表現力強化編

2020 年 4 月 10 日　第 1 刷発行
2023 年 3 月 20 日　第 2 刷発行

著　者　David E. Bramley

発行者　森　信久
発行所　**株式会社　松柏社**
〒 102-0072　東京都千代田区飯田橋 1-6-1
TEL　03 (3230) 4813　（代表）
FAX　03 (3230) 4857
http://www.shohakusha.com
e-mail: info@shohakusha.com

挿　　絵　うえむらのぶこ
装　　幀　小島トシノブ（NONdesign）
印刷・製本　日経印刷株式会社

略号 = 762

ISBN978-4-88198-762-9